ESTEBAN VICENTE

THE ARTISTOCRATIC EYE

essay by Irving Sandler

15 February – 17 March 2007

AMERINGER

YOHE

FINE ART

20 West 57th Street New York, New York 10019
tel: 212 445 0051 fax: 212 445 0102 www.ameringer-yohe.com

ESTEBAN VICENTE
THE ARTISTOCRATIC EYE

"I'm an American painter because I came to live in this country when I was young. But art transcends borders. I am considered an American painter yet my culture is Spanish forever."[1]
                                                                    Esteban Vicente

I met Esteban Vicente in the year or so before 1956, when I was employed at the Tanager Gallery, an artists' cooperative on Tenth Street in New York City. His studio was nearby, and taking a breather from his painting, he often would drop into the gallery. A young newcomer on the New York art scene, deficient in knowledge about contemporary art and its history, I learned a great deal from Vicente and was impressed by his serious and single-minded devotion to the art of painting. Until the very end of his life, in 2001, a week before his ninety-eighth birthday, he painted with unceasing energy, enthusiasm, and freedom. As he said: "I do what I like to do, and that is a blessing. So I am in competition with nobody—except myself."[2] All in all, Vicente became a role model to me.

Vicente's manner was dignified, proud, and elegant. He carried himself like a military man, like his father and grandfather who had served as officers in the Spanish army, as I later learned from old family photographs. But what struck me most was Vicente's courtly bearing, even in the shabby and rowdy surroundings of artists' venues, such as the Cedar Street Tavern or The Club, founded in 1949 by the Abstract Expressionists.

Although I knew that politically Vicente was a Republican who had been Spain's counsel in Philadelphia during the Civil War from 1937 (the year after arriving in the United States at age twenty-four) to 1939, I always imagined him as a grandee in the court of Philip IV, a friend of Velázquez or, at least, a sitter for one of his paintings, or even a stand-in for Velázquez himself.[3] Chuck Close, a friend and former student of Vicente's at Yale, viewed his professor in a more modern American light: "Movie star handsome, elegant beyond belief, and an extremely natty dresser (especially in contrast to the scruffy attire of the rest of the faculty), all the women students immediately fell in love with him. The male students were jealous."[4]

It is usually misguided to relate what one knows of an artist's life, personality, or temperament to his or her painting or sculpture. One's knowledge of an artist's life experience and psychic makeup is invariably too meager to connect it meaningfully to his or her art. Nonetheless, in the case of Vicente I cannot resist. Like the man, his painting is refined and graceful, and this, from the beginning of his career. Pedro Salinas, a poet friend of Vicente's in the 1920s, dubbed him "Vicente of the Aristocratic Eye," a characterization that remained true to the end of his life some eight decades later.[5]

●

1. Barbara Rose. "Interview with Esteban Vicente," January 1998, in *Esteban Vicente: Early Works* (New York: Ameringer Yohe Fine Art, 2004), p. 3.
2. Elizabeth Frank, *Esteban Vicente* (New York: Hudson Hills, 1995), p. 131.
3. Barbara Rose, in "Esteban Vicente and the New York School" (Huntington, NY: Heckscher Museum of Art, 2001), p. 28, suggested that Vicente the man is reminiscent of Velázquez's self-portrait in *Las Meninas*.
4. Chuck Close, "Tribute to Esteban Vicente," *Esteban Vicente: A Retrospective View: 1951-2000* (Scottsdale, AZ, and Santa Fe, NM: Riva Yares Gallery, 2002), p. 5.
5. Frank, *Vicente*, p. 13.

The paintings that made Vicente's reputation as a first-generation Abstract Expressionist date from 1950, shortly after he met the avant-garde painters and sculptors who lived in downtown New York. Prior to his "break-through," he had had a long and successful career as an artist in Barcelona, Madrid, and Paris. From 1921 to 1924, Vicente had received a thorough academic training at the Royal Academy of Fine Arts of San Fernando in Madrid. His study there enabled him to master "the tools" of art, but, as he said, his teachers had only one idea, "that one should follow what they believe is tradition and stick to it. It doesn't give you any ideas about anything," except, he added, "it prepares you to be against [the Academy]."[6] In Madrid, Vicente joined other artists and poets, who came to be known, in their resistence to cultural reactionaries, as the Generation of 1927, the *"putrefactos"* or "putrified ones," as the young radicals called them.[7] In 1929, Vicente's inclination toward Modernism led him to move to Paris, where he met the leading painters and sculptors and learned at firsthand of their art and culture.[8]

Esteban Vicente
Ramblas, 1931, oil on canvas,
21$\frac{1}{4}$ x 28$\frac{3}{4}$ inches, 54 x 73 cm
Private Collection

Vicente once wrote: "For me, the most powerful influence of the twentieth century in art is Cubism."[9] However, when he became an Abstract Expressionist, he rejected the constraints of Cubist design (while continuing to refer to it as a kind of pictorial stabilizer). He did so by painting directly and improvisationally in the manner that Harold Rosenberg termed Action Painting; Clement Greenberg, Painterly Painting; and myself, Gesture Painting. What engaged Vicente most about Gesture Painting was, as he said, "the idea that you don't know where you are going, you have to do it to find it."[10] Vicente and his friends maintained that the image encountered by an artist in the unpremeditated and subjective process of painting was a metaphor for "the self," and hence, the process was one of self-discovery. By its very nature, Gesture Painting focused on the artist because it was arrived at through an accumulation of paint marks dictated by what the painter believed to be an inner necessity.

What was the significance of self-revelation? As I view it, Vicente found the answer in recollecting the ideas of Miguel de Unamuno, a philosopher-novelist-poet, whom he had first encountered in the 1920s. Vicente so admired Unamuno that he would often go to the Madrid café frequented by Unamuno just to hear him talk.[11] Central to Unamuno's thinking was the belief "that when a man affirms his 'I,' his personal consciousness, he affirms man, *man concrete and real*, affirms the true humanism . . . and in affirming man he affirms consciousness"[12] (italics mine). As if glossing on Unamuno's words, in the talk "The Role of The Artist in Society" at Kent State University in 1982, Vicente said that the important questions were "What is the meaning of this man? What does he represent? How does he function?" He concluded that the artist's "activity as an artist is personal."[13] Or, as he said elsewhere: "Painting in the end . . . has to reflect the drama of the man and without that it's just craft."[14]

6. Frank, *Vicente*, p. 13.
7. Ibid.
8. A small paintings of lovers in a landscape, titled *Landscape with Red Umbrella* (1931) is prophetic in that it prefigures the contrasting pulls or tradition and Modernism in Vicente's abstractions. Strung across the foreground are barely visible electric wires. It is as if a sign of the modern age had impinged in a bucolic scene culled from a traditional *fêtes champêtre*, e.g., an early Goya.
9. Esteban Vicente, "Painting Should Be Poor," *Location*, vol. 1, no. 2, Summer 1964, p. 72.
10. Elizabeth Frank, "A Conversation with Esteban Vicente," *Esteban Vicente: A Forty Year Survey* (Guild Hall Museum, April 25-June 7, 1992), n.p.
11. Frank, *Vicente*, p. 14.
12. Miguel de Unamuno, *The Tragic Sense of Life* (New York: Dover, 1954), p. 13. First published in Spanish in 1912 and in English in 1921.
13. Esteban Vicente, "The Role of the Artist in Society," Kent State Lecture, 1982, unpublished. Reprinted in *Esteban Vicente 1999-2000: El Color Es La Luz* (Segovia, Spain: Museo de Arte Contemporáneo Esteban Vicente, 2001), p. 173.
14. Esteban Vicente, interview with Irving Sandler. *Smithsonian Institution, Archives of American Art.* August 26, 1968, p. 54.

Francisco José de Goya y Lucientes
Picnic on the banks of the Manzanares
1775, cartoon for a tapestry, canvas
107 x 116 inches, 272 x 295 cm, Cat.768
location: Museo del Prado, Madrid, Spain
photo credit: Erich Lessing / Art Resource, NY

15. Frank, "A Conversation with Esteban Vicente," n.p. Vicente considered himself an outsider but he was also a member of the Abstract Expressionist community. He also recognized, however, as he said in "On Painting and Painters: Notes and Comments 1960-1976," unpublished in *Esteban Vicente 1999-2000: El Color Es La Luz* (Segovia, Spain: Museo de Arte Contemporáneo Esteban Vicente, 2001), p. 168: "As an artist you have to be in a place where there are others. . . . Generally speaking, you need a stimulus." And that stimulus was "people with the same ideas, problems."

16. As if to stress his regard for the tradition of Western art, the images in a number Vicente's early Gesture Paintings resemble maps of Europe. It may not have been conscious on Vicente's part, but it is clear to me. The role that Spain plays in this image is also significant as in some pictures Vicente scrawls it out. This may have been his response to Franco's Spain.

17. Juan Manuel Bonet, "A Spanish Passion," *Descubrir el Arte*, January 2003, p. 19. Esteban Vicente, in an interview with Todd Granzow (in Frank, *Vicente*, p. 5) emphasized the European roots in his work by differentiating it from that of Clyfford Still. Still's painting, he said, did not have "the kind or refinement that is European, and which finally became the weakness of [his art]. . . . You cannot connect him with anything in Europe. No way."

18. Irving Sandler, notes of an interview with Landes Lewitin for a statement in "Is the Artist For or Against the Past," *Art News*, Summer and September 1958.

19. Vicente Todolí, "Esteban Vicente: On the Generation of 1927 and the New York School," *Esteban Vicente: Pinturas y Collages 1925-1985* (Madrid: Fundación Banco Exterior, 1987), p. 29.

20. Irving Sandler, "Conversations with de Kooning," *Art Journal*, Fall 1989, p. 216.

21. Clement Greenberg, *Partisan Review*, 1948.

22. Morton Feldman, *Art in America*, 1972.

23. Esteban Vicente, "Painting Should Be Poor," p. 68.

Improvisation enabled Vicente to avoid preconceived ideologies and ideas and to paint his experience directly. He was disposed to a trial-and-error method, since he was against dictation of any kind. As he put it, he was an "anarchist." When asked what that meant, he replied "to be free from any institution, or any convention either. Or authority, or dogma, or any group."[15] However, Vicente was not an out-and-out anarchist. Had that been the case, he would have rejected the past. He did not do so; indeed, he had a deep-rooted regard for the tradition of Western painting, and particularly that of Spain.[16] As he said, "We are in tradition and I would not exist without Zurbarán, Goya or Juan Gris."[17]

In acknowledging tradition, Vicente did not submit slavishly to its authority by aping past art. Instead, he embraced innovation with an eye to traditional aesthetic values of craft and quality; that is, he drew sustenance from the grand tradition's spiritual sap. He agreed with his friend Landes Lewitin, who said, "Avant-garde just means that an arrow is pointed to an added vision."[18] In fact, Vicente wanted to have it both ways— the freedom of improvisation as well as "intuitive control," the thoughtful care that the well-made work of art requires.[19] Vicente was the kind of artist, who, as de Kooning said about himself, was "grappling for a way to say something new. . . . I have this point of reference—my environment—that I have to do something about. But the Metropolitan Museum is also part of my environment. . . . I change the past."[20]

Avant-garde artists of Vicente's generation felt free to paint whatever they desired in part because they were subject to very few external pressures. Only a handful of dealers, critics, or curators were at all sympathetic or even interested in Abstract Expressionist painting—and there were hardly any sales. Most avant-garde artists lived in abject poverty; as Clement Greenberg wrote in 1948, what was real for the artists was "the shabby studio on the fifth floor of a cold-water, walk-up tenement . . .; the frantic scrambling for money; the two or three painters who admire your work; the neurosis of alienation that makes you such a difficult person to get along with. . . . The alienation of Bohemia was only an anticipation in nineteenth-century Paris; it is in New York that it has been completely fulfilled."[21] But artists voluntarily took vows of poverty and looked to their fellow artists for support and validation.

●

De Kooning, with whom Vicente shared a studio in 1950, showed him the way to Gesture Painting. At that time, Gesture Painting was still so new and experimental that, as Morton Feldman remarked, "for a brief moment . . . nobody understood art."[22] Who painted what first meant little to the pioneer Abstract Expressionists. They borrowed freely from one another and then repaid what they took with interest. What counted was painting that was personal and felt. As Vicente summed it up: "I believe that the only possibility of originality is personality, to be what you are. If one has personality, one is original."[23]

Esteban Vicente
In Pink and Gray,
1950, oil on canvas
41 x 51 inches, 104.1 x 129.5 cm
Collection of the Museo
Nacional de Arte Reina Sofía

Vicente's personality was very unlike that of de Kooning. In keeping with his temperament, de Kooning's painting was raw and aggressive. In contrast, Vicente's was lyrical. Whereas de Kooning prized the appearance of crudeness in his paintings, Vicente cultivated a beautifully painted look. The differences are clearly manifest in a comparison of two paintings of 1950, namely Vicente's *In Pink and Gray* (the first canvas he exhibited in New York), and de Kooning's *Excavation*. *In Pink and Gray* is composed of freely painted, irregular, distinct planar areas in a well-ordered composition. The brushwork is animate yet restrained, and the colors are muted and subtle. Weaving in and out of the color areas are freewheeling strips of black paint that lead the viewer through the painting. A counterpoint to the color areas, the linear components serve to create movement and fluidity as well as complexity and ambiguity. Atmosphere emanated by the grooves and ridges of the brushwork adds to the ambiguity. However, *In Pink and Gray*'s strongest impression is that of clarity, provided by the coherent design of the planar areas.[24] It announces the visual-poetry that would distinguish Vicente's painting thereafter.

In contrast to *In Pink and Gray*, *Excavation* is composed of aggressively brushed, harshly colored paint areas that interpenetrate in restless flux, evoking what W.H. Auden termed the Age of Anxiety. Whereas de Kooning's image refers to the hacked-up human body, as a kind of anatomical abstraction, Vicente's image evokes landscape, a poetic "interior landscape."[25]

Indeed, Vicente found Expressionism temperamentally alien. To him, it meant an excessive, generally aggressive or violent attack with the brush, which was supposed to signify uncontrolled emotion. He also denied that he was an Action Painter since he identified action with mindless spontaneity.[26] As he saw it, spontaneity and improvisation were different, the one out of control, the other in control. Vicente did value the freedom of Action Painting, but he was just as intent on self-discipline. In his improvisation, he welcomed upsurges of the unconscious but subjected them to conscious control. As he said, "To me, painting has to be done with your mind as clear as possible."[27] However, Vicente acknowledged that at one point in the process of painting there occurred a qualitative leap that the artist could not think back to.[28] In sum, Vicente was disposed to a "detached" and well-defined painting but one that was nonetheless "felt" and "personal." Because of his desire for clarity, he considered himself in the "classic" tradition of Western art, in contrast to "romanticism," of which the latest phase was "expressionism."[29] As for myself, I prefer José Maria Parreño's label of Vicente as a "classical anarchist."[30]

24. Frank, in *Vicente*, p. 35, offers another interpretation of *In Pink and Gray*. Stressing Vicente's roots in early twentieth-century tendencies, she wrote: "The painting itself solidly integrates two of Vicente's major allegiances: the Analytic Cubism of Picasso, Braque, and Gris, with its gridded infrastructure of interlocking planes, and that of Mondrian, whose 1913 abstraction, *Composition in Blue, Gray, and Pink*, is recalled both in the title and in the patches of subtle, almost transparant color."

25. Vicente, "Painting Should Be Poor."

26. Although Vicente disassociated himself from Action Painting, it strongly informed his improvisational process. As he said, in an interview with Elizabeth Frank in Bridgehampton, New York, in July 1980, "The idea is that first you put down anything, and this anything you put down is not related to any particular image but only to the limits of the canvas. And then when you put down the second thing the problem begins. The second thing you put should be related to the first one plus the limits again. That is when the thing begins to appear slowly. Only then, when it appears, maybe there is a possibility that there is some relation to something vague, something not precise, which only becomes precise as it gradually begins to appear on the canvas. Since the whole thing consists of making decisions all the time, these decisions convey finally the total. [I] put things in and take them out, change them until everything comes into place. [That] when you begin to have a corresponding feeling between the canvas and yourself." (Frank, *Vicente*, p. 27).

27. Frank, *Vicente*, p. 24.

28. Elizabeth Frank, "Interview with Esteban and Harriet Vicente," New York, February 6, 1980, in Archives of American Art, Esteban Vicente papers, no. 24. p. 11.

29. Dore Ashton, in "Esteban Vicente," *Arts Magazine*, March 1958, wrote that Vicente's "rejection . . . of baroque excess—a position leading to classicism— places him apart."

30. José Maria Parreño Velasco, "A Classical Anarchist," *Descubrir el Arte*, January 2003, p. 9. Mr. Parreño is Director of the Museo de Arte Contemporáneo Esteban Vicente, Segovia, Spain.

Willem de Kooning
American, 1904-1997, b. Netherlands,
Excavation, 1950, oil on canvas
81¼ x 101¼ inches, 206.2 x 257.3 cm,
Mr. and Mrs. Frank G. Logan Purchase Prize Fund;
gift of Mr. and Mrs. Noah Goldowsky and
Edgar Kaufmann, Jr., 1952.1
The Art Institute of Chicago.
photography © The Art Institute of Chicago.

31. Esteban Vicente, unpublished interview
with the artist with Todd Granzow, January
4, 1976.
In slowing down the action in his work,
Vicente may have in mind the state of
silence and serenity conveyed by
Chinese calligraphers—whose work he
admired—that informs the painting
process and is evoked in the completed
picture. Vicente owned several books of
Chinese calligraphy.

32. Vicente was steeped in the Spanish poet-
ry of his generation. He told Todoli that in
Spain he admired the poets of his gener-
ation more than the painters. He had in
mind such poets such as Federico García
Lorca, Juan Ramón Jiménez, Pedro
Salinas, Guillan, Alessandre, Alberti,
Cernuda, Altolaguirre, Gerardo Diego.
Jiménez, who was a lyrical poet, was par-
ticularly close to Vicente; he later got the
Nobel Prize. The poets would meet in
Vicente's studio to talk. The artists who
were friends of Vicente were Juan
Bonafé, Ramón Gaya, Pedro Flores,
Wladyslaw Jahl, and Benjamin Palencia.
Buñuel, the movie-maker, was also a
friend; Vicente saw him in Paris as well.

33. Sabastia Gasch, quoted in Juan Manuel
Bonet, "Esteban Vicente in His First
Landscape," *Esteban Vicente: Pinturas y
Collages 1925-1985* (Madrid: Fundación
Banco Exterior, 1987), p. 63.

34. Elizabeth Frank, "Interview with Esteban
and Harriet Vicente," p. 15. Vicente, on p.
17, added that Hans Hofmann and
Alexander Calder also had "joy."

Just as Vicente disliked Expressionist Sturm und Drang, he was averse to the immediacy of the allover "field" painting of Pollock, Still, Rothko, and Newman. The painting of these artists is experienced all at once because its design is non-relational, a kind of composition they considered non-Cubist, and hence radical. In contrast, Vicente's underlying organization is relational. Much as the forms are open, they are discrete, leading the viewer to read them slowly from part to part to whole. This kind of pictorial design had its source in the Synthetic Cubist images of Picasso, Braque, and Gris. Despite his departures from their painting, Vicente felt close to the Cubists, notably Gris.

Relational design enabled Vicente to slow down the "action" in his painting. Indeed, his canvases require prolonged viewing in order for them to be fully experienced. The spectator has to take his or her time. Indeed, the longer Vicente's painting is contemplated, the stronger and richer it becomes. He used a number of pictorial devices to decelerate the viewers' response. One was to float atmos-pheric color-forms gently in and out of focus. Another was to relate the forms so that some appear to be echoes, shadows, ghosts, or mirages of others in a kind of now-you-see-it-now-you-don't. Vicente discovered this mirage image in nature. He remarked to Todd Granzow that at sundown when the sun seems to sink into the ocean, at first it "doesn't look like a sphere. It's like an octagon. . . . And then, because the heat on the land and on the ocean affect the vision, so the [sun] is shimmering. . . . So then, finally, the sun sinks into the ocean, disappears. And what is left in the sky is a form the same as the sun, but green. It affects the eye that way."[31]

●

Vicente took what he needed from Abstract Expressionism, and, following his own bent, deflected it into something completely his own. What then was Vicente's artistic identity? In essence, he was a visual-poet whose painting was distinguished by its elegance, refinement, grace—in a word, beauty.[32] As early as 1931, the Barcelona crit-ic Sabastia Gasch wrote that Vicente's painting was "stated in a minor key, in a hushed voice, without a desire to cause stridency, nor to astound, nor to be dissonant."[33]

The beauty of Vicente's paintings is only part of their appeal. Many times there are also intimations of the tragic, notably, in the shadowy aspect of his colors—shrouded col-ors, specters of colors–subtle metaphors perhaps for death. Vicente was well aware of "the tragic sense of life," the title of Unamuno's most influential book. On the whole, how-ever, Vicente's temperament would not allow him to despair. A sign of this was his love of gardening—the sensuousness and sheer color of flowers, their energy as they impressed themselves on the eye and emotions. And above all, his gratification in the act of painting. He said that he had often heard painters talk of the pain they experience. He added, "it's true" but it was also "nonsense . . . I do what I enjoy."[34]

●

Hans Hofmann
Nocturn Glow, 1962, oil on canvas
48 x 36 inches, 122 x 92 cm
Collection of the Estate of Hans Hofmann

If Vicente's lyrical artistic temperament had little in common with the Abstract Expressionism of de Kooning and Kline, it was related to that of his peers William Baziotes, James Brooks, Philip Guston, Hans Hofmann, Bradley Walker Tomlin, and Jack Tworkov. In order to differentiate their painting and that of the Abstract Expressionists, critics coined the label Abstract Impressionism. Of course, most Abstract Impressionist painting had little if anything to do with that of Monet, Renoir, and their company. But the label stuck. By the middle 1950s, there were probably more Abstract Impressionists than Abstract Expressionists. This led the art historian Robert Goldwater to write that the defining mark of New York School painting had become its "concentration upon sensuous substance."

> With certain exceptions (of whom de Kooning is the most obvious) this is a lyric, not an epic art. [Here] are artists who like the materials of their art: the texture of paint and the sweep of the brush, the contrast of color and its nuance, the plain fact of the harmonious concatenation of so much of art's underlying physical basis to be enjoyed as such. They have become fine craftsmen with all the satisfaction that a craftsman feels in the controlled manipulation of his art, and all his ability to handle his medium so that his pleasure is transmitted to the beholder.[35]

Vicente obviously loved paint and painting, the physical manipulation of pigment, enabling him to create an astonishing variety of pictorial effects, ranging from heavy impastos to nuanced ethereal sprays and every effect in between, all of which added up to an embodiment of emotion.

The new American painters in the 1950s thought that their emphasis on the craft of painting was a "consolidation" of the innovations of the late forties. As John Ferren wrote in a much-discussed article in *Art News* (1955): "Consolidation is a conquest. . . . Abstract Expressionism has become more refined and relaxed, fewer nerves and more gray matter back of the eyes. In a word, better painted."[36] But without sacrificing spontaneity. Indeed, a critical issue was how to reconcile spontaneity with their preexisting knowledge of what it would yield. The solution was to try to have it both ways: by relying on intuition but amending it by exercising deliberate control in order to achieve "the intensity of the finished picture."[37]

Of his contemporaries, Vicente's painting was closest to that of Hofmann, an artist he admired. Their lives, too, had much in common, although Hofmann was more than two decades older than Vicente. As biographer and author Elizabeth Frank wrote: "Both came relatively late to the United States, knew the art of the museums intimately, had spent time in Paris (admittedly at very different times and among very different people), where they saw firsthand work by numerous modern masters."[38] Vicente also posed the same formal problem as Hofmann, as Vicente put it, "to create a form . . . that is not flat."[39]

35. Robert Goldwater, "Reflections on the New York School," *Quadrum8*, (Brussels, Belgium, 1960), p. 30.
36. John Ferren, "Stable State of Mind," *Art News*, May 1955, p. 23.
37. Ibid., p. 63.
38. Frank, *Vicente*, p. 22.
39. Frank, "A Conversation with Esteban Vicente," n.p.

Both artists developed painterly styles that had their source in Cubism and Fauvism, the seminal movements in the history of Modernist art. Moreover, Vicente and Hofmann used an improvisational "push and pull" to arrive at their images. However, Vicente's sensibility or artistic temperament was poles apart from Hofmann's. Whereas Hofmann was exuberant, Vicente was restrained. Hofmann's color tended to be highkeyed and bold; Vicente's was shadowy and nuanced.

●

In dealing with the development of Vicente's Abstract Expressionist painting, one must start with the collages he began to piece together in 1950, while teaching at the University of California at Berkeley. Indeed, the planar areas and their design in Vicente's paintings of the early fifties had their source in the torn papers from which he improvised

his collages.[40] His trial-and-error collage-making influenced not only his painting but remained central to his entire body of work; he would continue to create collages throughout his career.

Vicente considered painting and collage of a piece. As he wrote: "I think of collage, not as a separate, limited medium, but simply as a mode of painting. . . . The layers of paper are like the thin pigments of traditional oil painting but with the special luminosities and transparencies of this medium." Vicente conceived of tearing and scissoring paper as a form of drawing and the hand-colored swatches of paper as brushstokes. But there was a difference between collage and painting. In collage, as he said, "one must forget about the heroic qualities of oil painting. Collage as a medium seems to direct one towards intimacy of size and quality." However, in the end, Vicente required of collage "the quality of both concreteness and serenity that I find essential to my image of painting."[41]

The ease of moving pieces of colored paper around liberated Vicente's picture-making. He literally could revise at will. Consequently, the colors and shapes in the collages tend to be more varied and highkeyed than in the paintings. However, from 1956 to 1965, Vicente focused, in many of his collages, on black, commonly held to be the "color" of Spanish art.

It is difficult to classify the different periods in Vicente's painting stylistically since at any time he would be moving in a variety of directions. However, at the risk of being simplistic, the development of his painting entailed a progressive simplification and clarification of its components. From roughly 1950 to 1953, he made complex and active Gesture Paintings composed of a rich variety of freely painted color areas interspersed with linear elements that seem to be in perpetual, if slow-moving flux. In 1954, Vicente reduced and then suppressed the linear elements in his painting. He also condensed the varied forms of earlier paintings into roughly rectangular areas of massed brushstrokes with irregular edges. These canvases seem to synthesize Mondrian's abstract Cubist design and Matisse's Fauve color.

40. Collage as an art of cutting and pasting is somewhat related to construction sculpture, and it is noteworthy that Vicente began his career in art as a student of sculpture and would return to it late in life.

41. Esteban Vicente, Statement (New York: Grueunbaum Gallery, 1981), n.p. quoted in Frank, *Vicente,* p. 72. See also Esteban Vicente, "Collage as Painting," *It Is,* Spring 1958, p. 41.

They are related to Hofmann's work of the time but are brushier, less hardedged, and more sober and reserved. Several paintings call to mind windows and doors, possibly inspired, as Ellen Russotto, Consultant to the Esteban Vicente Catalogue Raisonné, has pointed out, by the facades of residences in Segovia, the Spanish city in which Vicente was born and grew up.[42] Other canvases, in which the blocky areas are dispersed in an atmospheric space, are reminiscent of farmhouses and barns in Castilian villages.

In 1959, the shapes in Vicente's paintings became more irregular, larger, and brushier. At this time, Vicente began to favor large color-forms, the infinitely variable design of which would be his essential compositional strategy throughout the remainder of his career. Around 1964, Vicente reduced the vigorous, gestural, open facture, simplified and enlarged the shapes even more than earlier work, and increasingly emphasized the interaction of colors. He retained relational design or structure, but his primary aim was to make color more ample visually and emotionally.[43] In 1965, Vicente reduced the brush-work more again by employing an air compressor and a spray gun, first for coloring the papers from which he was composing his collages and then for paintings on canvas, although he still continued to paint with the brush in many of his pictures.

By using an airbrush, Vicente could "reach a saturation of the color without the stroke . . . and without the thickness," as he said to me in 1968. It enabled him to heighten his color, refine his drawing, and more clearly articulate the structure. Airbrushing yielded stained "color shapes with absolutely sharp yet almost immaterial edges."[44] Staining pigment appealed to Vicente not only because it made color luminous and seem to vibrate and shimmer, but because it asserted the materiality of the thinned pigment and the canvas into which it was soaked. Staining also reduced the artist's autographic gesture or "touch," which calls attention to the creative process of the artist, and, consequently, is the primary Expressionist attribute. In sum, staining enabled Vicente to stress the purely visual effect of the saturated color. Indeed, expression-through-color became the dominant feature of his painting. Yet Vicente would not limit his pictorial means. In the middle 1980s, he began to vary staining with brushing pigment, and in 1996, he abandoned the spray gun.

In his attitude toward color as primary in painting, Vicente's thinking was reminiscent of that of Gauguin, who believed that in order for color to be fully felt visually and emotionally in its own right, elements that were alien to color had to be suppressed, notably complicated drawing, brushwork, and textures, and, above all, value contrasts.

The colors Vicente preferred throughout his long career were the issue of his subjective experience. As he said, "there are certain colors you identify with yourself."[45] He believed that critical aspects of the self are formed in early life and do not change.[46] Among the boyhood impressions that persisted in memory or dreams were the colors

Esteban Vicente
I, 1959, oil on canvas
40 x 32 inches, 101.6 x 81.3 cm
Collection of the Estate of Esteban Vicente

42. Ellen Russotto, "A Festival of Two Worlds: Esteban Vicente A Celebration on the Centennial of His Birth," *Centenario* (Madrid, Spain: Galeria Elvira Gonzalez, 2003), p. 78.
43. Staining thinned pigment into the canvas was a technique favored by younger artists, such as Morris Louis, Kenneth Noland, and Jules Olitski. However, unlike them, Vicente retained the relational structure that they rejected in favor of allover painting.
44. Elizabeth Frank, "Esteban Vicente Ripeness Is All," p. 5.
45. Undated interview, interviewer unknown, in Archives of American Art, Esteban Vicente papers, no. 17, p. 1.
46. Archives of American Art, Esteban Vicente papers, no. 21, p. 15.

Esteban Vicente
U, 1959, oil on canvas
38 x 32 inches, 96.5 x 81.3 cm
Collection of Sharon and John D.
Rockefeller IV

of the landscape around Segovia. Consequently, his palette was both "psychological" and "geographic." When I visited Segovia—with its omnipresent views of the arid Castilian plain—it occurred to me that the colors of the landscape constituted Vicente's essential palette. There were the same dry tans, browns, ochers, and yellows of the sun-beaten earth and the occasional farm; the off-yellows, at times tinged with muted pinks, of the dust-ridden atmosphere; the darker browns and umbers of plowed fields; the off-green hedges and bushes spotted here and there; and the off-blues and grays of the darkish shadows cast by of the spare flora and low hills and ridges.

Vicente's predilection for these colors reached back to his earliest paintings of the 1920s. It is also the palette of one of his Synthetic Cubist painting of the 1940s that was discovered recently (the other canvases of this decade were destroyed). It is significant that the tans, browns, ochers, umbers, and yellows were the colors favored in the 1920s by Vicente's brother Eduardo and his painter friends and acquaintances in Madrid, among them Lorenzo Aguirre, Juan Bonafé, Louis Garay, Pedro Flores, and Ramón Gaya. Earth colors also constitute the essential palette of Spanish master paintings through the ages, among them such Vicente favorites as the *bodegones*, saints, and still lifes by Velázquez, Zurbarán, Juan Sánchez Cotán, and Goya. Walking through the Prado I was surprised at how often the skies in Spanish pictures emanate a dusty yellow light even in heavenly visions; there is hardly a blue-blue to be seen. Similarly, when Vicente did use brighter colors, they tended to be "dusty."

For Vicente, the interaction of colors was meaningful only when it yielded a unifying allover light, *his* light, as it were. The search for this light was the purpose of his improvisational process of relating colors to one another. When Vicente discovered or recognized his light, the painting was "finished." Put another way, light was the signifier of Vicente's artistic identity.

Having arrived at a personal, pictorial vocabulary, Vicente put it through an extraordinary diversity of variations and permutations. Vicente was at one and the same time at ease in his "style" and eager to press beyond it. As he put it simply in a conversation with me in 1968: "You open a path and you go to a point and there you stop, and then from there is another path and it goes on forever."[47] John Ashbery wrote that in Vicente's painting, "shapes loom, condense, accumulate, dissolve, recur; color is a solid, a liquid, or a gas, floating, emerging, returning into itself, sometimes far back in the canvas, sometimes out in the room behind the spectator."[48] On the whole, the colors are sober and the facture nuanced. The color-forms seem to be in motion but their interactions are nonassertive and slow in tempo. The shapes gently approach or slither away, nudge, jostle, occasionally interpenetrate or melt into each other, or more accurately, as Elizabeth Frank commented, "drift and lock, lock and drift."[49]

47. Esteban Vicente, unpublished interview with Irving Sandler (East Hampton, NY, Smithsonian Institution, Archives of American Art, 1968).
48. John Ashbery, "Absence and Illusion," *Art News*, May 1972, p. 33.
49. Frank, *Vicente*, p. 91.

There is throughout Vicente's painting the sense that he gauged the scale of the color-forms, their placement, the intervals between them, and the rhythms they set up until their final "lock" perfectly embodied his artistic identity.

Frank summed up Vicente's late painting:

[It] is about the pleasure of freedom—the freedom that comes when you know your materials so well they have become an extension of yourself, and the freedom of being so thoroughly at home inside your formal language that you can let it take you wherever it wants to go. It is the freedom of knowing exactly who you are, and yet remaining open, as Vicente has remained open, to hidden reservoirs of memory, freedom, experience, and desire.[50]

Such was Vicente's sense of freedom that in his late paintings he would on the one hand verge toward a color field and on the other, toward a structured image, using organic as well as quasi geometric forms—with the emphasis always on color. In pictures such as *Space and Time* (1971), *Alison Series: Inner Light* (1976), and *Echo* (1979), he focused on structures composed of soft-edged, atmospheric rectangles of color. *Two Reds* (1986) emphasizes all-over reds. In any one year, say 1987, his paintings range from the somber mistiness of *Passage* to the brilliant but still misty oranges and reds of *Sifting*.

In the 1990s, Vicente's colors and forms on the whole became even more varied than in earlier work. The shapes in *Ariel* (1990) and *Consonance* (1991) call to mind multiple islands or oases. The palette ranges from the close-valued, predominantly green-blues of *Restful* (1990) to the blazing yellow on a reddish-orangish-purplish ground in an untitled canvas of 1993. All of these pictures are generally thinly painted to emanate a lambent light and serene atmosphere.

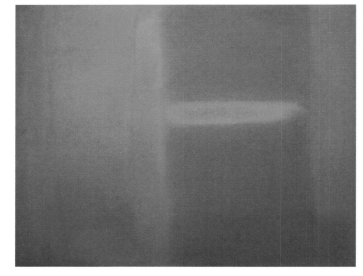

Esteban Vicente
Rushlight, 1979, oil on canvas
52 x 64 inches, 132.1 x 162.6 cm
Private Collection

●

Vicente lived in the United States for sixty-six years, from 1936 to his death, in 2001. He was certainly an American, but in critical ways he remained Spanish, and his Old World heritage entered into his art making. If he insisted that art has no nationality, he did allow that it has a cultural background. Consequently, his painting could both develop and flourish in an American avant-garde ambiance and retain references to its Castilian roots. As he said, "my mentality, the way I function, has to do with the fact that I was born in Spain. . . . And my way of thinking comes from there."[51]

National character or identity is extremely amorphous. It certainly is not innate, but it encompasses the values that a people cherish and aspire to live by (even if they fail). Spaniards I have talked with believe that a Spanish identity exists, and more specifically, that it is regional. When I asked Vicente Todolí, the director of Tate Modern, about his friend's Spanishness, he replied that Vicente was Castilian, "as Castilian as a chickpea."

50. Elizabeth Frank, "Introduction," *Esteban Vicente: Recent Works* (New York: Berry-Hill Galleries, 1989), n.p.
51. Elizabeth Frank, "A Conversation with Esteban Vicente," n.p.

Esteban Vicente
Composcion, 1963, oil on canvas
48 x 60 inches, 121.9 x 152.4 cm
Collection of Harriet Vicente

52. Elvira Gonzales, "A Sober Castilian," *Descubrir el Arte*, January 2003, p. 24.
53. Frank, "A Conversation with Esteban Vicente," n.p.
54. Esteban Vicente, "Gris: Reality Cubed," *Art News*, May 1958, p. 52, quoted in Frank, *Vicente*, p. 51.
55. Antonio Bonet Correa in "Modernity and Tradition in Esteban Vicente," *Zurbarán, Juan Gris, Esteban Vicente*, (Segovia, Spain: Museuo de Arte Contemporáneo Esteban Vicente, 2003), p. 28.
56. Unamuno, *The Tragic Sense of Life*, p. 1.
57. In Vicente, "Gris: Reality Cubed," pp. 30-32, Vicente spoke of the difficulties in explaining the drama of Gris' painting. He concluded: "Perhaps it is the drama of the man, the painter himself with his anxieties and the intensity of his search."
58. Esteban Vicente, interview with Todd Granzow, p. 7. In an essay on Zurbarán, in Correa, "Modernity and Tradition in Esteban Vicente," p. 28, Vicente wrote about the centrality of "plastic reality" in "the great tradition of Spanish painting," which in painting terms is defined by a denial of "illusion or fantasy" but informed by an instinctive regard for the "physicality of nature."
59. Vicente's regard for "poorness" also had a source in the Castilian landscape.
60. Esteban Vicente, "Painting Should Be Poor," p. 70.
61. Frank, *Vicente*, p. 91.
62. Ibid.

But how might that be defined? Elvira Gonzales, Vicente's friend and dealer in Madrid, wrote, "He was gifted with the *best qualities* of 'lo castellano': sincerity, honesty, pride, sobriety, self-demandedness, telling the truth even if that was not in his best interest"[52] (italics mine). None of this is verifiable, of course, but as metaphor it is meaningful, and in my opinion, it defines the Vicente I knew.

In Vicente's view, Spanish cultural identity was characterized by "a sense of reality."[53] As he said, with Juan Gris in mind: "Realism runs through all manifestations of art in Spain. In and through the work of Fray Luis de León, St. Teresa, Cervantes, Velázquez, Goya, [and] Picasso is found a concept of profound reality—a reality that springs from the play of the intellectual faculties and a sense for the material aspect of the world, a sense that is at the core of their artistic expression. And in painting, it is essential, it is elemental, to have this sense of the material aspect of the world."[54] Antonio Bonet Correa wrote that "In this regard there comes to mind here the famous remark by Santa Teresa de Jesús, who told her nuns that God lived among the kitchen pots."[55]

How to define *realism*? In Vicente's view, one must begin with the concrete individual or, in Miguel de Unamuno's words, the "man of flesh and bone, the man who is born, suffers, and dies—above all, who dies; the man who eats and drinks and plays and sleeps and thinks and wills; the man who is seen and heard."[56] But this concrete man has a spiritual dimension, which Unamuno insisted could be taken only on faith and not on reason. As I view it, Vicente's goal was to picture this singular individual, namely himself.[57] For him, the realistic portrayal of his features (such as those in innumerable portraits he had painted earlier in his career) could not reveal his true reality. Nor could this be disclosed through anecdote, fantasy, or theatrics, as in Surrealism, particularly that of his class-mate Salvador Dalí, which Vicente detested. Pointing to his exemplars, he said: "In Velázquez and Juan Gris [there] is no fantasy." No concealment or illusionism. "Everything is open."[58]

Vicente also thought that "poorness" was an attribute of the Spanish sensibility.[59] It was the humbleness of the paper that in part made collage an appealing medium for him. As for painting, he said: "I am after the sensuousness of the materials, but for me, painting has to be austere and somehow poor—poor in terms of means. I don't like luxurious painting. . . . By 'poor' I mean restrained, spare, meager. I am very anti-baroque."[60] The desire for a *estilo desornamentado* or "plain style"[61] caused Vicente to limit the number of forms and colors he used in each painting in order to condense or distill his imagery.[62] His aim was to achieve the maximum of expression with the minimum of means. Seeking humbleness also led him to work on a relatively modest, intimate scale—

in opposition to the aggressive "Big Picture," which came to be identified with Abstract Expressionism. Vicente believed that the Spanish artists he admired, above all Zurbarán and Juan Gris, about whom he wrote essays, also prized poorness and restraint and eschewed melodrama, opulence, and showiness.[63] He compared his own works to theirs: "there is a parallel in . . . austerity and sobriety, the asceticism, the silence . . . the intimacy, the enclosure . . . the artists' need to find themselves and their scale in the world." As scholar Edward J. Sullivan summed it up: "Vicente is in the tradition of the great Spanish painters Ribera, Zurbáran, and Velázquez, and the hallmarks of their painting are "restraint, subtlety, and understatement. . . . Vicente is not an artist of the grand gesture but of the meditative, carefully considered form."[64]

Ana Martínez de Aguilar, the previous director of the Museo de Arte Contemporáneo Esteban Vicente and the current director of the Museo Nacional Centro de Arte Reina Sofía, called my attention to the "Escorial Tradition" of Spanish art, exemplified by the restrained architecture of the Sixteenth-Century royal monastery of San Lorenzo de El Escorial, which she juxtaposed to the Spanish Baroque. The Escorial tradition, exemplified by Zurbarán, Velázques, and Cotán and, in the modern era, by Gris and Vicente, is austere and reflective, and avoids bombast and affectation. It is noteworthy that although Vicente admired Picasso, he preferred Gris.[65]

Vicente's realism had to be found in the materiality or reality of the painting medium, its colored pigment and the light that color emanates—in what he termed "the painting space."[66] He said: "The pigment is a very complicated thing. It works very much the same as sound in music. So you have to understand the material and have a feeling for it. . . . A painter has to deal with the material first [and] transform it into meaning."[67]

Vicente believed that painters have to start not only with the substance of the pigment but by feeling "the physicality of the world." He meant that artists did not have to paint specific things but rather the "sensation of physicality."[68] That was achieved through an "accumulation of experiences," which resulted in "an image."[69] These experiences "are related in a very vague sense to something you have seen somehow, but . . . not seen through the eye alone [but] what you have in yourself . . . through your whole sense." As Vicente's friend Andrew Forge commented about the internalization of the world by artists: "We look—we have always looked—for images, equivalences, out there in which we can discern our inner states. . . . What does any attribute of the outside world mean—what makes it worth commenting upon or . . . trying to re-create on any level, . . . if not by virtue of one's sense of connectedness to it? What does 'whole' or 'part' mean, or 'open' or 'closed,' or 'hard' or 'soft' if such qualities are not cited in truth to our own bodies and our sense of ourselves and our orientation to the world?"[70] Or, to quote Cézanne: "Nature is in the mind. Quality, light, color, depth which are there before us, are there only because they awaken an echo in our body and because the body welcomes them."

For Vicente the materiality of paint was a metaphor for the body, whose fate was death. At the same time, he hoped to transcend materiality/death by creating a sense of light that signified "the spirit." Vicente said: "I want to achieve luminosity

63. Vicente Todoli, in "Esteban Vicente: On the Generation of 1927 and the New York School," wrote that Vicente's painting referred most directly to that of Juan Gris. "He viewed Gris as the figure that updated a Spanish tradition present in Cervantes and Velázquez, in the literature of the mystics and in Zurbarán, Goya, and the philosophy of Unamuno, in the poetry of the 'Generation of 1927.'"
64. Edward J. Sullivan, "Esteban Vicente," *Esteban Vicente: The Painter* (Sante Fe, NM: Riva Yares Gallery, 1994), p. 7.
65. Ana Martínez de Aguilar, conversation with Irving Sandler, 2002.
66. Esteban Vicente, interview with Todd Granzow, p. 10.
67. Frank, *Vicente*, p. 48.
68. Esteban Vicente, interview with Robert Cordier, undated, Archives of American Art, Vicente papers, no. 18, p. 12.
69. Vicente, Archives of American Art, Vicente papers, no. 18, p. 12.
70. Andrew Forge, "On Painting," in *Critiques III* (New York: Cooper Union School of Art & Architecture, Fall 1974), pp. 57-59.

through opaque color."[71] Vicente's idea of a trans-material or "spiritual" light emanating from tangible matter is embedded in Catholicism. Vicente's father was a devout churchgoer and saw to it that his son was schooled by Jesuits. In his later life, Vicente became a lapsed Catholic, but acknowledged that his childhood indoctrination continued to influence his thinking and sensibility. Indeed, he retained indelible memories of the light in the halos around the heads of the holy family and saints, both in the churches and the Prado, to which his father took him regularly.

Vicente's conception of the body-spirit relationship is found in Catholic doctrine. In her review of Eleanor Heartney's *Postmodern Heretics: The Catholic Imagination in Contemporay Art*, Sue Taylor wrote that Heartney focuses on the Catholic teaching which declared "Christ both divine *and* fully human—that is, possessed of a physical body—in the doctrine of the Incarnation. Christ's resurrection was thus, in part, a corporeal event that foreshadowed the ultimate resurrection of all the dead, with the faithful reunited with their own bodies in a glorified state."[72] It is significant that the yearning for immortality and the conviction that the very body of the deceased would ascend to heaven was at the core of Unamuno's philosophy.

Catholic teachings as metaphors appear to have continued to inform Vicente's thinking. In time, he would suppress the religious connotations of light and formulate a secular variant he termed "the dream." As he said, "The most essential thing is to be able to dream. The only way to dream is by being aware of reality. . . . I mean by a sense of reality a notion of the physical aspect of the world that, by contact with an idea, transcends itself and becomes a dream. To dream, as Unamuno says, you have to be awake. It is the opposite of what people think, you have to dream with your mind open."[73]

●

Vicente developed his lyrical Abstract Expressionist style in the late 1940s, when beautiful painting was widely denigrated in the New York School. Tell an avant-garde painter that his or her work was elegant, handsome, or worst of all, decorative, and you would be shown the studio door. Letting all the scars and warts show was considered peculiarly relevant and American. *Beauty* was a put-down word, applicable to School of Paris painting. Willem de Kooning maintained that French artists had "some touch in making an object . . . that makes [it] look like a finished painting. They have a touch which I am glad not to have."[74] Vicente Todolí remarked that Vicente had that "touch."[75] As Elaine de Kooning summed it up: "'Beautiful' is a term that rarely can be applied to painting anymore. The struggle with oneself that now produces art is more likely to leave harsh, even ugly tracks."[76] This attitude changed in the 1950s, and Vicente played an influential role in ushering in the new lyrical abstraction. His painting, which embodies beauty in the best sense of that old-fashioned word, has come increasingly to be prized for its originality and masterliness.

●

Irving Sandler
2006

71. Vicente, "Painting Should be Poor."
72. The body in its concrete reality for all time to come is the basis of Vicente's friend Unamuno's metaphysic. His yearning for the immortality of the body—one's real body—that he made is the mainspring of his metaphysics.
73. Esteban Vicente, "Painting Should Be Poor," p. 72.
74. Willem de Kooning, in Robert Goodnough (editor), "Artists' Sessions at Studio 35," *Modern Artists in America* (New York: Wittenborn Schultz, 1951), p. 13.
75. Vicente Todolí, in "Esteban Vicente: On the Generation of 1927 and the New York School", p. 29, with de Kooning's rejection of "finish" in mind, commented: "Vicente, on the other hand, had this touch and was interested in this very 'finished' quality."
76. Vicente recognized what Elaine de Kooning was saying. In Elizabeth Frank, Interview, New York, November 27, 1982, Archives of American Art, Esteban Vicente papers, no. 29, p. 29, he said: "Beauty was terrible. Ugliness was the thing."

Untitled
1950, oil on paper on panel, 16 x 12 inches, 40.6 x 30.5 cm

Untitled
1950, oil on canvas, 40 x 50 inches, 101.6 x 127 cm
Collection of Beth Rudin Dewoody

No. 24

1950, oil on canvas, 39 x 32 inches, 99.1 x 81.3 cm

Untitled
1952, drawing, ink on paper, 22^{3}/$_{8}$ x 28^{1}/$_{2}$ inches, 56.8 x 72.4 cm

Y
1959, oil on canvas, 32 x 40 inches, 81.3 x 101.6 cm

Untitled
1960, oil on canvas, 28 x 26 inches, 71.1 x 66 cm

Ate
1960, oil on canvas, 49 x 37 inches, 124.5 x 94 cm

Siva
1960, oil on canvas, 38 x 50 inches, 96.5 x 127 cm

Ochre, White, Gray and Blue (Teresa)
1961, collage on paper, 28 x 38 inches, 71.1 x 96.5 cm

No. 1 (also written with an added zero: No. 10)
1961, oil on canvas, 48 x 60 inches, 121.9 x 152.4 cm

Untitled
1962, collage with ink drawing, 11 x 12 inches, 27.9 x 30.5 cm

Untitled
1962, oil on canvas, 36 x 49 inches, 91.4 x 124.5 cm

Black, Red, & Gold
1964, collage on paper, 24 x 30 inches, 61 x 76.2 cm

Untitled
1965, collage, paper on board, 20 x 28 inches, 50.8 x 71.1 cm

Black Susan
1968, collage, paper on board, 60 x 40 inches, 152.4 x 101.6 cm
Collection of Harriet Vicente

Untitled
1970, charcoal drawing, 16 x 12 inches, 40.6 x 30.5 cm

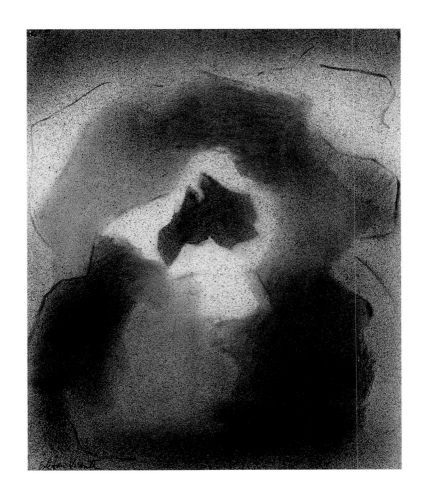

Untitled
1971, charcoal and ink on paper, 16³/₄ x 13¹/₂ inches, 42.5 x 34.3 cm

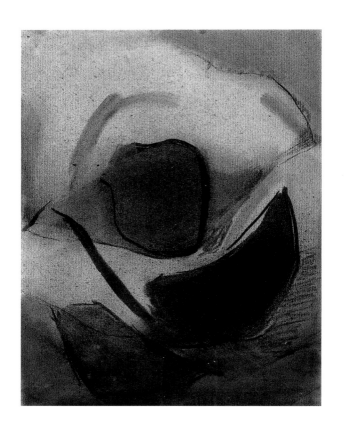

Untitled
1972, drawing, charcoal and acrylic spray, 12³/₄ x 9³/₄ inches, 32.4 x 24.8 cm

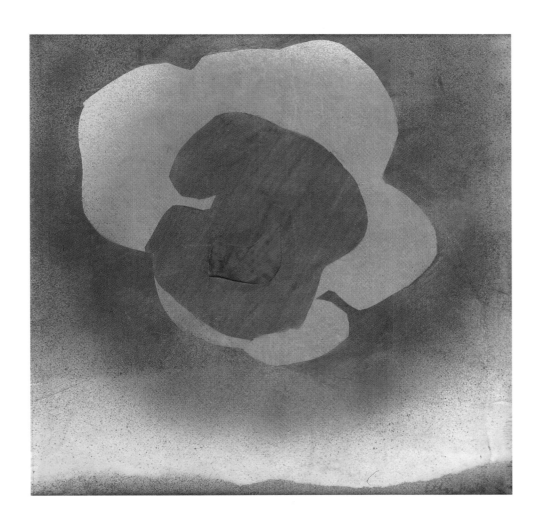

Happy Birthday Harriet 1972
1972, collage, 22 x 22 inches, 55.9 x 55.9 cm

Untitled
1980, drawing, pastel on paper, 16 x 17^{1}/$_{2}$ inches, 40.6 x 44.5 cm

Untitled
1980, acrylic on paper, 22$\frac{1}{4}$ x 18$\frac{3}{4}$ inches, 56.5 x 47.6 cm

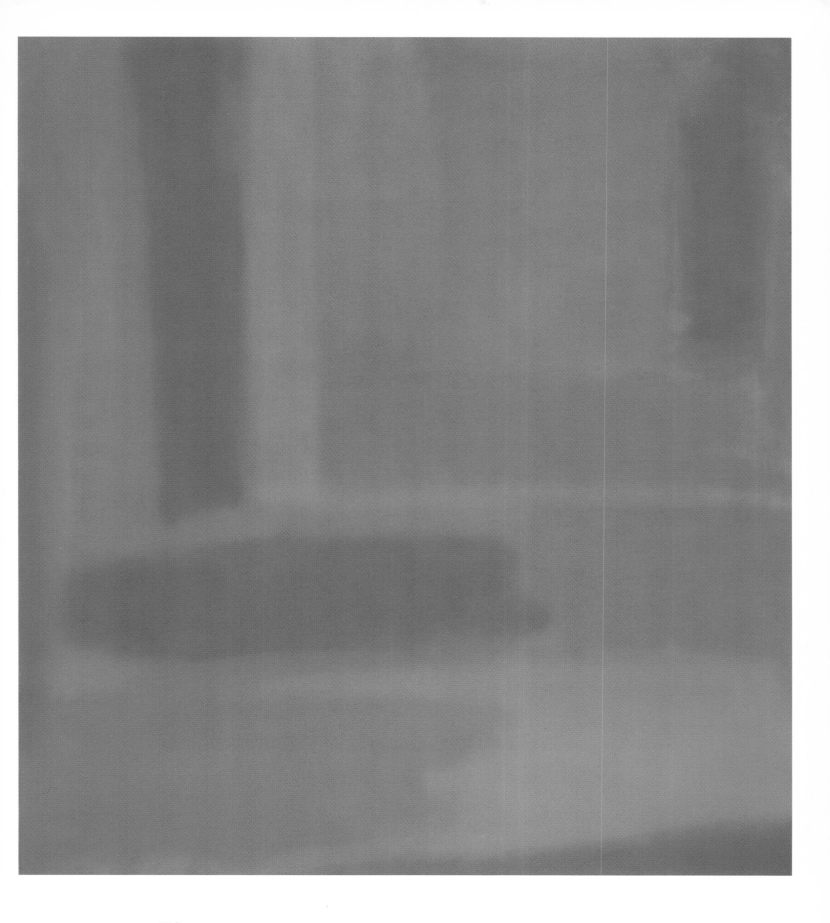

Midsummer
1980, oil on canvas, 68 x 60 inches, 172.7 x 152.4 cm

Colour Transitions
1986, oil on canvas, 36 x 45 inches, 91.4 x 114.3 cm

Midsummer
1980, oil on canvas, 68 x 60 inches, 172.7 x 152.4 cm

Primavera Series: Red Form
1985, collage, paper on canvas, 34 x 32 inches, 86.4 x 81.3 cm

Untitled
1985, collage on paper, 28 x 36 inches, 71.1 x 91.4 cm

Colour Transitions
1986, oil on canvas, 36 x 45 inches, 91.4 x 114.3 cm

Red Across
1986, oil on canvas, 64 x 52 inches, 162.6 x 132.1 cm

Untitled
1988, collage with ink and pencil drawing on board, 11³/₄ x 16¹/₂ inches, 29.8 x 41.9 cm

Untitled
1989, collage on paper on canvas, 26 x 34 inches, 66 x 86.4 cm

Untitled
1990, drawing, acrylic and pastel on paper, 20$\frac{1}{2}$ x 35$\frac{1}{2}$ inches, 52.1 x 90.2 cm

Untitled
1991, oil on canvas, 44 x 62 inches, 111.8 x 157.5 cm

Untitled
1992, oil on canvas, 48 x 62 inches, 121.9 x 157.5 cm

Untitled

1992, collage, paper on canvas, 40 x 30 inches, 101.6 x 76.2 cm

Untitled
1994, collage, paper on canvas, 17 x 17 inches, 43.2 x 43.2 cm

Harmony
1995, oil on canvas, 50 x 42 inches, 127 x 106.7 cm

Country Side
1997, oil on canvas, 52 x 42 inches, 132.1 x 106.7 cm

Simetria
1998, oil on canvas, 42 x 52 inches, 106.7 x 132.1 cm

Corola
1999, oil on canvas, 42 x 52 inches, 106.7 x 132.1 cm

CHECKLIST

Untitled
1950, oil on paper on panel
16 x 12 inches, 40.6 x 30.5 cm
Estate inventory #P50-07

Untitled
1950, oil on canvas
40 x 50 inches, 101.6 x 127 cm
Estate inventory #P50-06
Collection of Beth Rudin Dewoody

No. 24
1950, oil on canvas
39 x 32 inches, 99.1 x 81.3 cm
Estate inventory #P50-01

Untitled
1952, drawing, ink on paper
22³/₈ x 28¹/₂ inches, 56.8 x 72.4 cm
Estate inventory #D52-04

Y
1959, oil on canvas
32 x 40 inches, 81.3 x 1016. cm
Estate inventory #P59-12

Untitled
1960, oil on canvas
28 x 26 inches, 71.1 x 66 cm
Estate inventory #P60-03

Ate
1960, oil on canvas
49 x 37 inches, 124.5 x 94 cm
Estate inventory #P60-08

Siva
1960, oil on canvas
38 x 50 inches, 96.5 x 127 cm
Estate inventory #P60-01

Ochre, White, Gray and Blue (Teresa)
1961, collage on paper
28 x 38 inches, 71.1 x 96.5 cm
Estate inventory #C61-08

No. 1 (also written with an added zero: No. 10)
1961, oil on canvas
48 x 60 inches, 121.9 x 152.4 cm
Estate inventory #P61-01

Untitled
1962, collage with ink drawing
11 x 12 inches, 27.9 x 30.5 cm
Estate inventory #C62-20

Untitled
1962, oil on canvas
36 x 49 inches, 91.4 x 124.5 cm
Estate inventory #P62-03

Black, Red, & Gold
1964, collage on paper
24 x 30 inches, 61 x 76.2 cm
Estate inventory #C64-02

Untitled
1965, collage, paper on board
20 x 28 inches, 50.8 x 71.1 cm
Estate inventory #C65-11

Black Susan
1968, collage, paper on board
60 x 40 inches, 152.4 x 101.6 cm
Estate inventory #C68-07
Collection of Harriet Vicente

Untitled
1970, charcoal drawing
16 x 12 inches, 40.6 x 30.5 cm
Estate inventory #D70-06

Untitled
1971, charcoal and ink on paper
16³/₄ x 13¹/₂ inches, 42.5 x 34.3 cm
Estate inventory #D71-01

Untitled
1972, drawing, charcoal and acrylic spray
12³/₄ x 9³/₄ inches, 32.4 x 24.8 cm
Estate inventory #D72-06

Happy Birthday Harriet 1972
1972, collage
22 x 22 inches, 55.9 x 55.9 cm
Estate inventory #C72-01

Untitled
1980, drawing, pastel on paper
16 x 17¹/₂ inches, 40.6 x 44.5 cm
Estate inventory #D80-25

Untitled
1980, acrylic on paper
22¹/₄ x 18³/₄ inches, 56.5 x 47.6 cm
Estate inventory #D80-02

Midsummer
1980, oil on canvas
68 x 60 inches, 172.7 x 152.4 cm
Estate inventory #P80-01

Primavera Series: Red Form
1985, collage, paper on canvas
34 x 32 inches, 86.4 x 81.3 cm
Estate inventory #C85-18

Untitled
1985, collage on paper
28 x 36 inches, 71.1 x 91.4 cm
Estate inventory #C85-04

Colour Transitions
1986, oil on canvas
36 x 45 inches, 91.4 x 114.3 cm
Estate inventory #P86-05

Red Across
1986, oil on canvas
64 x 52 inches, 162.6 x 132.1 cm
Estate inventory #P86-16

Untitled
1988, collage with ink and pencil drawing
on board
11³/₄ x 16¹/₂ inches, 29.8 x 41.9 cm
Estate inventory #C88-08

Untitled
1989, collage on paper on canvas
26 x 34 inches, 66 x 86.4 cm
Estate inventory #C89-04

Untitled
1990, drawing, acrylic and pastel on paper
20¹/₂ x 35¹/₂ inches, 52.1 x 90.2 cm
Estate inventory #D90-11

Untitled
1991, oil on canvas
44 x 62 inches, 111.8 x 157.5 cm
Estate inventory #P91-29

Untitled
1992, oil on canvas
48 x 62 inches, 121.9 x 157.5 cm
Estate inventory #P92-28

Untitled
1992, collage, paper on canvas
40 x 30 inches, 101.6 x 76.2 cm
Estate inventory #C92-10

Untitled
1994, collage, paper on canvas
17 x 17 inches, 43.2 x 43.2 cm
Estate inventory #C94-14

Harmony
1995, oil on canvas
50 x 42 inches, 127 x 106.7 cm
Estate inventory #P95-43

Country Side
1997, oil on canvas
52 x 42 inches, 132.1 x 106.7 cm
Estate inventory #P97-56B

Simetria
1998, oil on canvas
42 x 52 inches, 106.7 x 132.1 cm
Estate inventory #P98-47B

Corola
1999, oil on canvas
42 x 52 inches, 106.7 x 132.1 cm
Estate inventory #P99-25B

SELECTED MUSEUM COLLECTIONS

Albright-Knox Art Gallery, Buffalo, NY

Art Institute of Chicago, Chicago, IL

Australian National Gallery, Canberra, Australia

Baltimore Museum of Art, Baltimore, MD

Berkeley Art Museum, University of California, Berkeley, CA

Blanton Museum of Art, University of Texas, Austin, TX

The Brooklyn Museum, Brooklyn, NY

The Butler Institute of American Art, Youngstown, OH

The Corcoran Gallery of Art, Washington, DC

Dallas Museum of Arts, Dallas, TX

Delaware Art Museum, Wilmington, DE

Detroit Institute of Arts, Detroit, MI

Grey Art Gallery, New York University, New York, NY

Guild Hall Museum, East Hampton, NY

Harvard University Arts Museums, The Fogg Art Museum, Cambridge, MA

Herbert F. Johnson Museum of Art, Cornell University, Ithaca, NY

Hirshhorn Museum and Sculpture Garden, Smithsonian Institution, Washington, DC

Honolulu Academy of Art, Honolulu, HI

The Hood Museum of Art, Dartmouth College, Hanover, NH

Institut Valencià D'Art Modern, Valencia, Spain

Los Angeles County Museum of Art, Los Angeles, CA

Metropolitan Museum of Art, New York, NY

Museo de Arte Contemporáneo Esteban Vicente, Segovia, Spain

Museo Nacional Centro de Arte Reina Sofía, Madrid, Spain

Museum of Contemporary Art, Chicago, IL

Museum of Fine Arts, Boston, MA

The Museum of Modern Art, New York, NY

National Museum of American Art, Smithsonian Institution, Washington, DC

The Nelson-Atkins Museum of Art, Kansas City, MO

Neuberger Museum of Art, State University of New York, Purchase, NY

New Jersey State Museum, Trenton, NJ

The Newark Museum, Newark, NJ

Palm Springs Desert Museum, Palm Springs, CA

The Parrish Art Museum, Southampton, NY

Patrimonio Nacional, Madrid, Spain

Princeton University Art Museum, Princeton, NJ

The Rose Art Museum, Brandeis University, Waltham, MA

San Francisco Museum of Modern Art, San Francisco, CA

Smith College Museum of Art, Northampton, MA

Solomon R. Guggenheim Museum, New York, NY

Tucson Museum of Art, Tucson, AZ

UCLA at the Armand Hammer Museum of Art and Cultural Center, Grunwald Center for the Graphic Arts, Los Angeles, CA

Wadsworth Atheneum, Hartford, CT

Walker Art Center, Minneapolis, MN

Weatherspoon Art Museum, University of North Carolina at Greensboro, NC

Whitney Museum of American Art, New York, NY

Worcester Art Museum, Worcester, MA

Yale University Art Gallery, New Haven, CT

CHRONOLOGY

1903
Born Esteban Vicente Pérez on January 20 in Turégano, Province of Segovia, Spain. He is the third of six children born to Toribio Vicente Ruíz and Sofía Pérez Álvarez. His father is a commissioned military officer who paints for pleasure. His brother, Eduardo, will also become a painter.

1903-1920
In order to educate his children in Madrid, Vicente's father resigns his military position and takes an administrative position at the Banco de España. The family lives in an apartment on Ronda de Atocha, near the Prado Museum and the General Hospital. From the age of four, Vicente regularly accompanies his father on visits to the Prado. Attends a Jesuit school.

1920
Enters the military academy; leaves after three months.

1921-1924
At age 18 enrolls in the Real Academia de Bellas Artes de San Fernando in Madrid and spends three years studying sculpture. Salvador Dalí is a fellow student. Receives an award to travel in the Province of Castile to visit historical sites and study works of art; briefly expelled for insubordination. In 1922, 1923, and 1924 he spends summers in Murcia, an eastern province of Spain.

1924-1927
Shares a studio on Calle del Carmen with James Gilbert, his first American friend. Both artists turn to painting; their friendship lasts until Gilbert's death in the 1970s. Moves to a studio on the Paseo del Prado. Develops friendships with poets associated with the "Generation of 1927": Federico García Lorca, future Nobel laureate Juan Ramón Jiménez, Rafael Alberti, Jorge Guillén, Pedro Salinas, as well as future filmmaker Luis Buñuel, publisher Ernesto Giménez Caballero, painters Juan Bonafé, Francisco Bores, and Wladislaw Jahl, from Poland. The studio becomes a meeting place for intellectual and artistic discussion attended by poets who come daily, knowing they

are likely to see Juan Ramón there. Vicente admires José Gutiérrez Solana, an older painter whose work follows the traditions of the masters. His landscape, figure and still life drawings are reproduced in the literary magazines *Mediodía* in Seville, and *Verso y Prosa*, published in Murcia by Juan Guerrero. Reads and admires the great Spanish philosopher, Miguel de Unamuno.

1928
First one-man exhibition of paintings at the Ateneo de Madrid is commented upon in Juan Guerrero's book, *Juan Ramón de Viva Voz*. Leaves Madrid for Paris, where he lives in a hotel until he takes a studio that he invites painter Pedro Flores to share. Joaquín Peinado, a Spanish painter, becomes a friend. Supports himself by retouching photographs and working on theatre sets for the Folies Bergère. Visits Picasso in his studio at Rue la Boetie, above Galerie Paul Rosenberg; Picasso, already familiar through magazine reproduction with Vicente's work, warns him against returning to Spain. Exhibits in the *Salon des Surindependents*, Place Versailles.

1929
Meets a young American, Michael Sonnabend, later a New York art dealer, who remains a lifelong friend. French critic Maurice Reynal mentions his work in a review of the *Salon des Surindependents* in Paris; his work is also reviewed in *Paris Soir*. Leaves Paris and spends six months in London, frequently visiting painter Augustus John and his circle.

1930-1934
Invited 1930 to exhibit work in Barcelona, where he lives for the next year and a half; his studio is at Arribau 222, studio number 13. Travels to Majorca. His dealers are Joan Merli, a great supporter of modernism in the arts, and Montse Isern of Galeries Syra. One-man exhibition at Galería Dalmau includes scenes of Barcelona life: flamenco dancers and guitarists, boats and the port, outdoor cafes and the Ramblas. Sebastiá Gasch writes the catalogue introduction for exhibition at Galeria Avinyó. Included again in the *Salon de Surindependents* in Paris. In 1930

left to right: Esteban Vicente in the lap of his mother. Sofía Pérez y Álvarez, his father, Toribio Vicente y Ruíz, his sister and brother. Turégano, Spain. c.1903-1904. Esteban Vicente aged 5-7 years. Probably Madrid, Spain. c.1908-1910. Esteban Vicente at the Real Academia de Bellas Artes de San Fernando. Madrid, Spain. c.1921-23 Esteban Vicente. c.1920-1921. Esteban Vicente with Magdalena Bonafé, the sister of Juan Bonafé, in La Alberca. Murcia, Spain. 1924-1928.

60

and 1934, exhibits in Spain in El Heraldo de Madrid. The Junta para la Ampliación de Estudios in Madrid awards him a scholarship to study abroad, affording him the opportunity to return to Paris in 1932. In Paris takes a studio at 147 Rue Broca where he also lives; meets the Surrealist artist Max Ernst through English friend, Darcy Japp. Paintings and drawings included in numerous one-man and group exhibitions in Barcelona between 1931-1934.

1935
In Barcelona marries Esther Cherniakofsky Harac (dit Estelle Charney), an American student at the Sorbonne, whom he meets in Paris. They live in Ibiza, a small island off the coast of Spain, for eight months during which Vicente works from nature making small drawings, watercolors, and paintings.

1936
After deciding to move to New York City, is in Madrid for a farewell family visit when on July 18th the Civil War breaks out. Volunteering for the Loyalist cause, he is told that there is not enough ammunition and assigned the job of painting camouflage on military vehicles in the mountains near Madrid. After again requesting active duty, he is told that he will be more useful to the Loyalist cause in the United States, and departs with his wife for New York. Lives on Minetta Lane in Greenwich Village, a few doors away from sculptor José de Creeft, whom he had known in Barcelona and Paris, and with whom he remains friends until de Creeft's death in 1983.

1937
Daughter Mercedes born. First one-man exhibition in New York City at the Kleemann Galleries, showing still lifes and figures, many painted on Ibiza; the exhibition is reviewed in Art News. The first American painter he meets is Joseph Stella, with whom he forms a lasting friendship. Develops a friendship with painter/critic Walter Pach, who later translates the journals of Delacroix into English; Pach writes catalogue essay for Kleemann exhibition. Fernando de los Ríos, Ambassador from Spain to the United States, asks Vicente to accept post in Philadelphia as Vice-Consul of the Republic of Spain, a post he holds until the end of the Spanish Civil War in 1939.

1938
The Spanish Institute in New York City honors painters Esteban Vicente, José López Mezquita, and sculptor José de Creeft for their outstanding contributions to the fine arts. Summers in Martha's Vineyard, Massachusetts, painting figures and landscapes.

1939-1940
Lives with wife and daughter on Bleecker Street in Greenwich Village, with studio on 15th Street near Fifth Avenue. Meets and forms a close friendship with composer Edgar Varèse, who resides nearby on Thompson Street. Becomes an American citizen. Art News reviews his second exhibition at Kleemann Galleries of figure studies, portraits, and landscapes made in France and Spain.

1941
Accepts his first invitation to be included in a major American group exhibition at the Pennsylvania Academy of Fine Arts in Philadelphia. At Bonestell Gallery in New York City exhibits portraits, figures, and landscapes painted in Martha's Vineyard and Pennsylvania.

1942-1945
Supports himself through portrait commissions and teaching Spanish at City College and the Dalton School in New York City. Also works for the Bureau of War Information. His daughter Mercedes dies of a congenital heart ailment. Following divorce, in 1944 marries María Teresa Babin, a poet and professor of Spanish language and literature. They live at 280 Hicks Street in Brooklyn; he maintains a studio at 43 Greenwich Street in Greenwich Village. His first one-man exhibition of Cubist-inspired paintings and drawings is held at the Ateneo Puertorriqueño in Puerto Rico. Pedro Salinas writes the introduction to the catalogue. Also exhibits at the University of Puerto Rico, where he shows representational works from 1934-1945, as well as recent abstract paintings.

Esteban Vicente working on a sculpture; horns drawn on model's head, seated at left. c.1922-1924. Esteban Vicente retouching photographs. Paris, France. 1928
Esteban Vicente with Magdalena Bonafé, the sister of Juan Bonafé, seated 2nd from left, and Juan Bonafé's mother, seated far right. La Alberca. Murcia. Spain. 1924-1927.

1946
Teaches painting at the University of Puerto Rico. His second one-man exhibition at the Ateneo Puertorriqueño, devoted solely to abstract paintings, is reviewed in *Pincel y Paleta*.

1947-1949
Returns to New York City; lives and works at 138 Second Avenue. Teaches Spanish in the evenings at City College. Develops a close friendship with composer Stefan Wolpe and his wife, writer/poet Hilda Morley. Meets and forms lasting friendships with many seminal New York School artists: painters Willem de Kooning, Jackson Pollock, Mark Rothko, Franz Kline, Barnett Newman, sculptors Philip Pavia, Ibram Lassaw, as well as critics Harold Rosenberg and Thomas B. Hess. In 1949, while teaching painting over the summer at the University of California at Berkeley, he makes his first collage. His drawing illustrates the cover of *El Autógrafo* by Jorge Campos.

1950
Establishes a studio at 88 East 10th Street, later sectioning off a part of his floor as a studio for Willem de Kooning. With its artist tenants and galleries, Tenth Street becomes famous as the center of the downtown New York art world. Art historian Meyer Schapiro and critic Clement Greenberg select Vicente, now aged 47, for inclusion in the important *Talent 1950* at the Kootz Gallery. Also selected to exhibit in the Annual exhibition at the Whitney Museum of American Art and has a one-man exhibition at Peridot Gallery, where painters James Brooks and Bradley Walker Tomlin also exhibit. Elected a voting member of The Club, a weekly forum organized by Philip Pavia for exchanges among artists, critics, and distinguished guests. Establishes closer contact with many artists, including painters John Graham, Ad Reinhardt, Balcomb Greene, Elaine de Kooning, Mercedes Matter, Aristodemos Kaldis, Jack Tworkov, Al Copley and sculptors David Hare and George Spaventa.

1951
Participates in the celebrated *9th Street* exhibition. Included in critic Thomas B. Hess's book, *Abstract Painting: Background and American Phase*, the first definitive volume on the New York School. Included in the first group exhibitions of New York School art sent to France and Japan. As summer art director of the Highfield Art School in Massachusetts, organizes panel discussions and exhibitions of New York School artists, including Willem de Kooning, Giorgio Cavallon, Franz Kline and Al Copley among others. Included in *Art News* article "The Year's Best" by editor Alfred Frankfurter.

1952
Included in the *Pittsburgh International Exhibition*, Carnegie Institute, and *Aspects of American Painting*, Sidney Janis Gallery, New York and Galerie de France, Paris.

1953
Elaine de Kooning's article "Vicente paints a collage" appears in *Art News*. The Stable Gallery in New York City continues the New York School focus of the *9th Street* exhibition with the Stable Annual; Vicente is included every year through 1957. One-man exhibitions at Allan Frumkin Gallery, Chicago, and the California Palace of The Legion of Honor, San Francisco. Teaches at Black Mountain College where colleagues include composers Stefan Wolpe, John Cage, dancer Merce Cunningham, poet Robert Creeley; painter Dorothea Rockburne is his student. Forms close and lasting friendship with painter William Baziotes.

1955
One-man exhibition at Egan Gallery, whose roster includes Willem de Kooning, Jack Tworkov, Franz Kline, Giorgio Cavallon, sculptors Joseph Cornell and Reuben Nakian. Included in numerous group exhibitions. Begins to spend weekends and summers in the Hamptons.

1957
One-man exhibition at Rose Fried Gallery, which also shows Kurt Schwitters, El Lizzitsky, Jean Arp, Marcel Duchamp and Sonia Delaunay. The cover of the February issue of *Art News* features a Vicente collage.

Esteban Vicente, seated at right, with Juan Bonafé, seated 2nd from left, in Murcia, Spain. c.1923-1924. Esteban Vicente. 1924-1928. Esteban Vicente and Pedro Flores. Paris, France. 1928. Photo from J.P. Crespelle, Montparnasse Vivant, Librairie Hachette, Paris, 1962, p.303. Photo: uncredited.

1958

One-man exhibition of drawings at Leo Castelli Gallery. Thomas B. Hess reviews his exhibition at Rose Fried Gallery in *Art News*: "Esteban Vicente paints in the high tradition of the Masters..." Meets Harriet Godfrey Peters, an active art collector of that period. Thomas B. Hess asks him to write an article on Juan Gris for *Art News*, concurrent with the Gris exhibition at the Museum of Modern Art; his article, "Gris: Reality Cubed", appears in the May issue. *It Is* magazine, published by Philip Pavia, prints Vicente's statement on collage.

1959

Harold Rosenberg, writing in *Art News Annual*, includes Vicente as one of the "leaders in creating and disseminating a style... (that) constituted...the first art movement in the United States." Thomas B. Hess focuses on Vicente in an article in *Art News* titled "The Year's Best: 1958". First one-man exhibition at André Emmerich Gallery in New York. Accepts a position at New York University, where he continues teaching until 1968. Included in *the Pittsburgh International Exhibition*.

1961

One-man exhibition at the Walker Art Center in Minneapolis, Minnesota; his works are also included in major group exhibitions in the Museum of Modern Art, The Whitney Museum of American Art, the Solomon R. Guggenheim Museum, The Carnegie Institute, the Seattle World's Fair, and the 6th International Exhibition, Tokyo, Japan. Receives a Ford Foundation Purchase Award. After divorce from wife Teresa, marries Harriet Godfrey Peters and moves to Gramercy Park in New York City; continues to maintain his studio on 10th Street.

1962

Thomas B. Hess again selects him for "The Year's Best" in *Art News*; feature article on Vicente is published in *Newsweek* magazine. Awarded a fellowship to the Tamarind Lithography Workshop in California; produces numerous editions of prints. Teaches at the University of California at Los Angeles; sculptor Tony Berlant is his student. His paintings and collages are included in *American Vanguard Art*, exhibition at American Embassy in London; *Pictures on Exhibit*, group show organized by the International Council of the Museum of Modern Art and circulated to twelve Latin American countries, singles out his work.

1963

A provocative exchange of sentiments and opinions between Vicente and Robert Motherwell regarding the Spanish Republic is published in "Editor's Letters" in *Art News*. While teaching at Yale University meets young painters Chuck Close, Janet Fish, and Brice Marden. Painter Susan Crile studies with Vicente at New York University.

1964

Along with Mercedes Matter, Charles Cajori and George Spaventa, Vicente becomes a founding member of the New York Studio School of Drawing, Painting and Sculpture. He and wife, Harriet, purchase summer home in Bridgehampton, Long Island, where he sets up a studio and they begin creation of wild and cultivated flower garden. Publishes an article titled "Painting Should be Poor" in *Location Magazine*. His work is featured on the cover of the January issue of *Art International*.

1965

Artist-in-residence at Princeton University, where he begins to use an air compressor and spray gun to color papers used in collages; later he will use this technique with paintings on canvas. Travels to Mexico with Harriet.

1966

Travels to Morocco with Harriet. Included in numerous group exhibitions across the United States.

1967

Death of close friend Ad Reinhardt. Vicente's work is included in *American Collages*, an exhibition organized by the Museum of Modern Art that travels in Europe.

Esteban Vicente and Michael Sonnabend on board ship. Paris, France. 1929. Esteban Vicente, seated at center, and Estelle Charney, seated at right on sand. Barcelona, Spain. 1930s. Egan Gallery, New York, 1954, Esteban Vicente far left, Ibram Lassaw, Theodore Brenson, Franz Kline, Willem de Kooning, Charles Egan, Jack Tworkov.

1969
Artist-in-residence at the Honolulu Academy of Fine Arts where he has a one-man exhibition. Included in a major exhibition organized by curator William Rubin at the Museum of Modern Art titled *The New American Painting and Sculpture: The First Generation*. Returns to Princeton University as artist-in-residence.

1970
Work by Vicente exhibited at the American Academy and Institute of Arts and Letters in New York City.

1972
Poet John Ashbery, in an article on Vicente in *Art News*, notes that he is "widely known and admired as one of the best teachers of painting in America." Moves to Hotel des Artistes at 1 West 67th Street, a world-renowned artists' residence since the turn of the century. Travels again to Morocco with Harriet.

1973
Teaches painting at Columbia University.

1974
Beloved stepdaughter Alison Peters dies.

1975
Accompanies Harriet on Jain pilgrimage to India. Continuing friendships with Meyer Schapiro, John Ashbery, artist Saul Steinberg, sculptor Costantino Nivola. Included in *Collages* exhibition at Betty Parsons Gallery in New York City.

1976
Designs cover for *Street Magazine* commemorative issue on Black Mountain College.

1977-1979
Travels to Egypt and Israel with Harriet. Artist-in-residence at the University of New Mexico at Albuquerque.

1980
Elected Associate National Academician at the National Academy of Design in New York City.

1981
Award candidate at the American Academy and Institute of Arts and Letters.

1982
Travels to Turkey with Harriet. Included in *The Americans: The Collage*, Contemporary Arts Museum, Houston, Texas.

1983
Moves his studio to 529 West 42nd Street. Awarded the Benjamin Altman Prize by the National Academy of Design.

1984
Receives Honorary Doctorate of Fine Arts from Parsons School of Design, New York City.

1985
Awarded the Saltus Gold Medal by the National Academy of Design. Also, recipient of an award from the American Academy and Institute of Arts and Letters, citing him as "one of the most gifted of the first generation of Abstract Expressionist painters... with "a sensibility created in Europe for the express purpose of opening the eyes and ears of Americans to the peculiar beauty around them." Visiting artist-in-residence at the National Academy of Design and the Vermont Studio School. Travels in Spain with Harriet and writer Elizabeth Frank to retrace his Spanish roots for a monograph.

1986
Awarded the title of National Academician by the National Academy of Design.

1987
Esteban Vicente: Pinturas y Collages 1925-1985, a retrospective exhibition curated by Natacha Seseña, is held in Madrid at the

Esteban Vicente. Bridgehampton Studio, New York. 1991. Photo credit: Laurie Lambrecht. Wolf Kahn and Esteban Vicente attending the Members Dinner at the American Academy of Arts and Letters. New York City. April 8, 1997. Photo credit: Dorothy Alexander. Esteban Vicente. Spain. August 1991.

Fundación Banco Exterior. Develops friendships with Egyptologist Bernard Bothmer and writer William Maxwell. Included in *Leo Castelli y sus artistas*, Centro Cultural Arte Contemporáneo, Mexico City.

1988
Receives the Childe Hassam-Eugene Speicher Purchase Award from the American Academy and Institute of Arts and Letters.

1989
Death of his friend Elaine de Kooning.

1991
Receives Spain's highest award, the Gold Medal of Honor in the Arts, presented by King Juan Carlos and Queen Sofía at the Prado in Madrid. Turégano, the town of his birth, names a street after him.

1992
Travels to Spain to be present at the opening of his one-man exhibition at Palacio Lozoya, Segovia, to commemorate Spain's entry into the European Community.

1993
Celebrates his 90th birthday. Elected a member of the American Academy of Arts and Letters; awarded Honorary Doctorate of Fine Arts from Long Island University, Southampton College. Guild Hall Museum, East Hampton, Long Island, presents him with a Lifetime Achievement in the Arts Award.

1994
On occasion of his 91st birthday, the New York Studio School of Drawing, Painting and Sculpture exhibits a selection of his recent paintings.

1995
Retrospective exhibition of his collages, curated by Vicente Todolí, is held at IVAM Centre Julio González in Valencia, Spain; travels to the Patrick and Beatrice Haggerty Museum of Art at Marquette University in Milwaukee, Wisconsin. Monograph by Elizabeth Frank is published.

1996
Travels to Spain. Moves into new studio adjoining residence at 1 West 67th Street; abandons use of the spray gun in his painting.

1997
Established in his new studio, he produces 20 paintings in three months. Death of his longtime friend Willem de Kooning; he writes a tribute for *ABC*, a major Spanish newspaper.

1998
Esteban Vicente. Obras de 1950 a 1998 opens at the Museo Nacional Centro de Arte Reina Sofía in Madrid then travels to other venues in Spain: Santiago de Compostela, Valladolid, Palma de Majorca. Receives the Premio Castilla-León de las Artes Award in Valladolid. Spanish Government honors him with a new museum in Segovia, the Museo de Arte Contemporáneo Esteban Vicente. Holds his last session of student critiques at the New York Studio School as he has done consistently for thirty-five years.

1999
Both he and Harriet receive Spanish Government award, the Gran Cruz de la Orden Civil de Alfonso X, El Sabio, for their contributions to art. Receives the Segovia Man of the Year Award and El Premio Arcale from the city of Salamanca. Continues to work daily in his studios in New York City and Bridgehampton.

2000
For the first time, he does not spend the winter in his New York studio; remaining in Bridgehampton. Continues to paint and draw, completing his last work in September 2000.

2001
Dies at home in Bridgehampton on January 10, surrounded by family and friends. His ashes are interred in the garden of the museum in Segovia named in his honor.

Esteban Vicente receiving Gold Medal for the Fine Arts from King Juan Carlos of Spain. Prado Museum, Madrid, Spain. July 3, 1991. Esteban Vicente. Madrid, Spain. March 1994. Esteban Vicente in his Bridgehampton studio. 1994. Esteban Vicente with his "toys." Bridgehampton, New York. 1992. Photo credit: Renate Pfleiderer.

SELECTED BIBLIOGRAPHY

Anderson, Wayne, *American Sculpture in Process: 1930-1970*, New York Graphic Society, Boston, MA, 1975, p. 86.

Arnason, H. H., *History of Modern Art*, 3rd Edition, Harry N. Abrams, New York, 1986, p. 394.

Arte en España 1918-1994, Alianza Editorial, S.A., Madrid, Spain, 1995, pp. 19, 29, 34, 44, 455-456, 468, illus. pp. 153, 154, 248, 399, 400.

Ashbery, John, *Reported Sightings: Art Chronicles 1957-1987*, Alfred A. Knopf, New York, 1989, pp. xii, xiv, xvi, 103, 203-208, 215, 312.

Ashton, Dore, *The New York School: A Cultural Reckoning*, Viking Compass Books, New York, 1973, p. 212.

Ashton, Dore, *The Unknown Shore: A View of Contemporary Art*, Little, Brown, and Co., Boston, MA, 1962, pp. 86, 87, illus. p. 88.

Babin, María Teresa, *Fantasia Boricua*, Las Americas Publishing Co., New York, 1956, p. 1, illus. pp. 9, 17, 43, 51 ,61, 71, 87.

Babin, María Teresa, *La Hora Colmada*, Santander, 1960, title page, illus. on cover.

Benezit, E., *Dictionnaire des Peintures, Sculpteurs*, Nouvelle Edition, Librairie Grund, Paris, France, 1976, Tome no. 10, p. 490.

Bonet, Juan Manuel, *Diccionario de las Vanguardias en España (1907-1936)*, Alianza Editorial, Madrid, Spain, 1995.

Bulletin, Weatherspoon Gallery Association, University of North Carolina at Greensboro, 1972, p. 4.

Bulletin, Weatherspoon Gallery Association, University of North Carolina at Greensboro, 1973-1974, p. 11.

Catalogue Raisonné Tamarind Lithography Workshop, 1960-1970, University of New Mexico Art Museum, Albuquerque, 2004, pp. 259, 260, illus. p. 259-60.

Clarkson, Austin, *On the Music of Stefan Wolpe*, Pendragon Press, Hillsdale, NY, 2003, pp. 20, 107, 109, 110, 339, cover illus.

Colección Amigos del Centro de Arte Reina Sofía, Museo Nacional Centro de Arte Reina Sofía, Madrid, Spain, 1989, pp. 230-31, color illus.

Colección Arte Contemporáneo, Association "Colección Arte Contemporáneo," Madrid, Spain, 1991, pp. 15, 123, 125, 304, 306, 308, 496, 503, illus. pp. 305, 307, 309.

Colección Municipal de Arte Contemporáneo Pintura y Escultura, Ayuntamiento de Madrid, Spain, May 1999, pp. 32, 299, illus. p. 256.

Collection of Mr. and Mrs. Ben Heller, Museum of Modern Art, New York, 1961, illus.

Crespelle, J.P., *Montparnasse Vivant*, Librairie Hachette, 1962, p. 303.

Cummings, Paul, *Dictionary of Contemporary American Artists*, 4th Edition, St. Martin's Press, New York, 1982, pp. 19, 571.

Cummings, Paul, *Dictionary of Contemporary American Artists*, 5th Edition, St. Martin's Press, New York, 1987.

Diehl, Gaston, *The Moderns: A Treasury of Painting Throughout the World*, Crown Publishing, New York, n.d., pp. 194, 216.

Digby, John and Joan, *The Collage Handbook*, Thames and Hudson, London, 1985, pp. 212-13, illus. p. 213.

Dorival, B., *Peintres Contemporains*, Mazenod, Paris, 1964.

DuPont, Diane C., and Katherine Church Holland, Garna Garren Muller, and Laura L. Sueoka, *San Francisco Museum of Modern Art: The Painting and Sculpture Collection*, Hudson Hills Press, New York, 1985, illus. p. 386.

Esteban, P., *Guia Museo Nacional de Arte Reina Sofía*, Madrid, Spain, 1994, p. 118.

Fehr, Michael, and Stanford Wurmfeld, (editors), *Seeing Red*, Salon Verlag, Cologne, Germany, 2004, pp. 15, 42, illus. pp. 39, 45.

Feiffer, Jules, "Esteban Vicente," *Proceedings of the American Academy of Arts and Letters*, Second Series, no. 52, New York, 2001, pp. 106-109.

Fernandez-Cid, Miguel, "Una Conversacion Entrecortada," *Kalias Revista D Arte*, año VI, num. 11, Semeste 1, 1994, IVAM Centre Julio González, Valencia, Spain, 1994, pp. 60-63, illus. pp. 61, 62, 63.

Frank, Elizabeth, *Esteban Vicente*, Hudson Hills Press, New York, 1995.

Geldzahler, Henry, *New York Painting and Sculpture 1940-1970*, E.P. Dutton & Co., New York, 1969, p. 32.

Guerrero Ruiz, Juan, *Juan Ramon de viva voz*, Insula, Madrid, Spain, 1961, pp. 83, 252, 268, 311.

Harris, Mary Emma, *The Arts at Black Mountain College*, MIT Press, Cambridge, MA, 1988, pp. 20, 232.

Herskovic, Marika (editor), *American Abstract Expressionism of the 1950s: An Illustrated Survey*, New York School Press, New York, New Jersey, 2003, pp. 346, 349, 372, illus. pp. 347, 348.

Herskovic, Marika (editor), *New York School Abstract Expressionists: Artists Choice by Artists*, New York School Press, New Jersey, 2000, pp. 8, 10, 12, 16, 20, 24, 26, 39, 52, 53, 370, 373, 393, illus. pp. 371, 372.

Hess, Thomas B., *Abstract Painting: Background and American Phase*, Viking, New York, 1951, p. 142, illus. p. 143.

Hess, Thomas B., "Introduction," *The Artist's World*, Shapolsky Publishers, New York, pp. 11-12.

Hess, Thomas B., *Willem de Kooning*, George Braziller, New York, 1959, p. 31.

Hess, Thomas B., *Willem de Kooning*, Museum of Modern Art, New York, 1969, p. 73.

Hunter, Sam, *Art Since 1945*, Harry N. Abrams, New York, 1958, pp. 306, 326.

Hunter, Sam, *Modern American Painting and Sculpture*, Dell Books, New York, 1959, p. 160.

Janis, Harriet, and Rudi Blesh, *Collage: Personalities, Concepts, Techniques*, Chilton Book Co., Philadelphia and New York, 1962, pp. 159, 160, 171, illus. nos. 212, 213.

Johnson, Ken, "Las Abstracciones Apolineas de Vicente," *Kalias Revista D Arte*, año VI, num. 11, Semestre 1, 1994, IVAM Centre Julio González, Valencia, Spain, 1994, p. 40, illus. p. 41.

Junoy, Josep Maria, *L'Actualitat Artistica*, Barcelona Libreria, Catalonia, Spain, 1931, p. 84.

The Leo Book ICI Salutes Leo Castelli, ICI Leo Awards Benefit Publication, p. 14.

Lowry, W. McNeil, *The Arts and Public Policy in the United States*, Prentice-Hall, Englewood Cliffs, NJ, 1984, unpaginated.

McDarragh, Fred W., *The Artist's World in Pictures*, E.P. Dutton & Co., New York, 1961, pp. 12, 83, 87.

Mediodía XI Revista de Sevilla, Seville, Spain, March 1928, two illus., unpaginated.

Modern Artists in America, Wittenborn Schultz, New York, 1951.

Mones, Arthur, *Artists in Photographs*, Horizon Press, New York, 1981, p. 25.

Motherwell, Robert, and Ad Reinhardt (ed. Assoc.), *Modern Artists in America*, no. 1, Wittenborn Schultz, New York, 1951, p. 116, illus. p. 85.

Muñoz, Miguel Angel, *El Origen de la Niebla*, Ediciones Andromeda, San Jose, Costa Rica, 2003, p. 5.

Muñoz, Miguel Angel, *Lineas Paralelas*, Editorial Praxis, Mexico DF, 2000, p. 9, illus. cover and pp. 10, 12, 14, 16, 18, 20, 22, 24, 27, 28.

Muñoz, Miguel Angel, *Yunque de sueños 12 artistas contemporáneos*, Editorial Praxis, Mexico DF, 1999, pp. 23-29, illus. pp. 30, 31.

The Museum and Its Friends, Whitney Museum of American Art, New York, 1958, entry no. 170, illus. p. 56.

Myers, D. H., *The Thursday Evening Art World*, McCall Publishing, New York, 1970, p. 106.

O'Connor, Francis V., *Jackson Pollock*, Museum of Modern Art, New York, 1967, pp. 60, 64, 68.

Osborne, Harold (editor), *The Oxford Companion to Twentieth-Century Art*, Oxford University Press, Oxford, England, 1981, p. 571.

"Presentation of Awards . . . of the American Academy of Arts and Letters," *Proceedings*, Second Series, no. 36, The American Academy and Institute of Arts and Letters, New York, 1985, p. 24.

Regards sur la Peinture Americaine, Galerie de France, Paris, 1952, entry no. 29.

Rose, Barbara, *American Art Since 1900*, Frederick A. Praeger, New York, 1967, p. 206.

Rosenberg, Harold, *The Anxious Object: Art Today and Its Audience*, Horizon Press, New York, 1964, pp. 50, 83, 208, illus. p. 121.

Rosenberg, Harold, *Artworks and Packages*, Dell Publishing, New York, 1969, p. 146.

Rosenberg, Harold, *Arshile Gorky: The Man, The Time, The Idea*, Sheepmeadow Press/Flying Point Books, New York, p. 22.

Rosenberg, Harold, *Art and Other Serious Matters*, University of Chicago Press, 1985, p. 243.

Rubin, William S., *The New American Painting and Sculpture: The First Generation*, Museum of Modern Art, New York, 1969.

Rumaker, Michael, *Black Mountain Days*, Black Mountain Press, Asheville, NC, 2003, pp. 243-45.

Sandler, Irving, *The New York School*, Harper & Row, New York, 1978.

Santamaria, Juan Manuel, *Arte en Segovia Siglo XX*, Caja de Ahorros y Monte de Piedad de Segovia, Spain, 1985, p. 44, illus. p. 43.

Serraller, Francisco Calvo, *España: Medio Siglo de Arte de Vanguardia 1939-1985*, Fundación Santillarre, Ministerio de Cultura, Madrid, Spain, 1986, pp. 30-31.

Seuphor, Michel, *Dictionnaire de la Peinture Abstraite*, Hazan, Paris, 1957.

Stevens, Mark, and Annalyn Swan, *De Kooning: An American Master*, Alfred A. Knopf, New York, 2004, pp. 331, 336, 372, 398, 410, 431.

Verso y Prosa: Boletin de la Joven Literatura, no. 10, Murcia, Spain, October 1927, unpaginated. illus.

Wescher, Herta, *Collage* (translated by Robert E. Wolf), Harry N. Abrams, New York, 1963, p. 307.

The Whitney Review, Whitney Museum of American Art, New York, 1960-1961, unpaginated, illus.

Esteban Vicente's 67th Street studio in New York. Photo credit: Ellen Russotto.

AMERINGER

YOHE

FINE ART

Published on the occasion of the exhibition

ESTEBAN VICENTE
THE ARTISTOCRATIC EYE
15 February – 17 March 2007

Ameringer & Yohe Fine Art
20 West 57th Street
New York, New York 10019
tel: 212 445 0051 fax: 212 445 0102

Photography credits:
Color plates by Jordan Tinker
Personal photos © Estate of Esteban Vicente

Catalogue designed by HHA Design, New York
Printed by Paola Gribaudo, Torino, Italy

Publication copyright © 2007 Ameringer & Yohe Fine Art
All rights reserved

ISBN: 0-9776071-9-4